T0193370

THIS BOOK IS DEDICATED TO

JOHNNELL GRAY

"Who's encouragement

and understanding

has renewed my hope."

THE ADVENTURES OF
TULIE RIDGE
SERIES PRESENTS

<u>Tulie Ridge and the</u>
<u>Snowman</u>

Written and Illustrated by
BRIGITTE RENEE COMER

AuthorHouse™
1663 Liberty Drive
Bloomington, IN 47403
www.authorhouse.com
Phone: 833-262-8899

Because of the dynamic nature of the Internet, any web addresses or links contained in this book may have changed since publication and may no longer be valid. The views expressed in this work are solely those of the author and do not necessarily reflect the views of the publisher, and the publisher hereby disclaims any responsibility for them.

Any people depicted in stock imagery provided by Getty Images are models, and such images are being used for illustrative purposes only. Certain stock imagery © Getty Images.

This book is printed on acid-free paper.

ISBN: 978-1-4389-1024-6 (sc)

Library of Congress Control Number: 2014906722

Print information available on the last page.

Published by AuthorHouse 01/15/2024

author HOUSE®

Tulie Ridge and the Snowman

"The Adventures of The Tulie Ridge Series"

Written and Illustrated by

Brigitte Renee Comer

Tulie Ridge lived on a farm with her mother and father and baby brother, Jeremy.

1

Tulie's mother liked baking cakes and pies for the family.

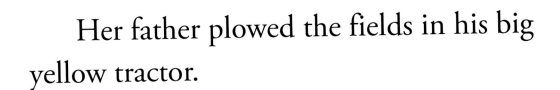

Her father plowed the fields in his big yellow tractor.

And Tulie's little brother, Jeremy was just a happy little baby, who played most of the day.

Tulie Ridge had all sorts of adventures. Today, she and her father would go outside in the snow to make a snowman.

Tulie was so excited, she could not stop smiling.

After breakfast, Tulie's mother gave
her a carrot, two blue buttons and seven
red cranberries

Tulie didn't know why her mother would give her such strange things, but she put the blue buttons, the carrot and the red cranberries into her pockets anyway.

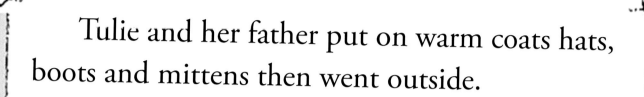

Tulie and her father put on warm coats hats, boots and mittens then went outside.

The snow was very white and very cold in her little red mittens.

Tulie had lots of fun making snow angels by lying on her back in the snow and waving her arms and legs back and forth.

Tulie and her father played games in the snow.

She even made a snow fort to hide behind when they threw snowballs at each other. It was great fun!

When they finished playing, Tulie helped her father gather snow and roll it into a big ball. This would be the snowman's feet.

They made a second ball, rolling it around until it was almost as big as the first one, but not quite as big.

They put this one on top of the bigger one and this would be the snowman's body.

Then they made a third ball, rolling it until it was the size of a basketball. They put this one on top of the body.

This would be the snowman's head.

The snowman was looking great!

Tulie and her father used two sticks for the snowman's arms and some rocks for buttons on his shirt.

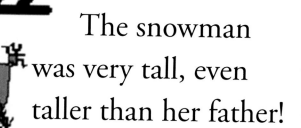

The snowman was very tall, even taller than her father!

Her father thought the snowman was finished.

But Tulie thought something was missing.

She looked hard at the snowman.

He didn't have any eyes! How could he
see the pretty white snow without eyes?

Then Tulie remembered the blue buttons
her mother had given her.

She gave them to her father to put them in the snowman's face to make eyes. He could see now!

Tulie was very happy. But something was still missing…

He didn't have a nose! How would he smell the good food that Tulie's mother was cooking for dinner?

Tulie pulled the carrot from her pocket.

Tulie pushed the carrot in where every snowman's nose should be. But still there was something missing…

Where was the snowman's mouth? If he didn't have a mouth how else would he be able to smile to show how happy he was to have someone make him?

The seven red cranberries were the last things in her pocket.

Tulie thought they would make a great smiling mouth and put them on the snowman's face.

19

Tulie was so pleased, she danced around the snowman and sang a happy song.

Her father danced around the snowman too, smiling and laughing.

Soon it became too cold for Tulie and her father to stay outside.

Tulie wondered if the snowman would be cold standing out in the yard all day without warm clothes.

So, Tulie's Father gave the snowman his hat and scarf.

At last the snowman was finished.

To Tulie, the snowman's smile seemed even happier.

22

Tulie Ridge, her mother, her father and her little baby brother, Jeremy, admired the snowman standing in the front yard through the window until it was time for dinner.

Before going to bed, Tulie checked the window one more time.

The snowman was still there, seeing out of blue button eyes, smelling with a carrot nose, smiling a happy red cranberry smile and wearing her father's hat and scarf.

That night, Tulie Ridge fell asleep very tired and but also very happy she and her father had played outside in the snow and made the snowman.

Enjoy Other Titles in the Adventures of Tulie Ridge Series

Written by Brigitte Renee Comer

- *Tulie Ridge and the Popsicle Man*

- *Tulie Ridge and the Lost Puppy*

- *Tulie Ridge and the Little Christmas Tree*

- *Tulie Ridge and the First Day of School*

- *Tulie Ridge Goes to the Pumpkin Patch*

- *Tulie Ridge and Valentine's Day Cards*

- *Tulie Ridge and the Easter Egg Hunt*

- *Tulie Ridge and the Thanksgiving Day Dinner*

- *Tulie Ridge and the Surprise Birthday Party*

- *Tulie Ridge Learns How to Swim*

About the Author

Brigitte Renee Comer was born in Washington, DC and currently leads a very productive existence dividing her time working as a full time computer administrator, part time driver's education instructor and sound assistant with several local Jazz and R&B bands. She also, has working patent projects for several insightful inventions.

Although, this is the first in a series of children's books she has published, Ms. Comer has written many fun stories, some depicted from her own childhood

and adult experiences. Her colorful life has enhanced her insight to delightful description and illustrated creations which entice the imagination of both young and old.

After studying under a literary institute, her latest venture has been to pursue a diversified writing career which encompasses several literary areas of interest; including, but not exclusive of; children's literature, poetry and romance.

Her relaxation hobbies include: swimming, gardening, reading, crochet, knitting, jewelry design, sewing, dancing, watching movies, and playing with her three dogs.

Ms. Brigitte Renee Comer plans to release more children's books, poetry and romance novels in the very near future.

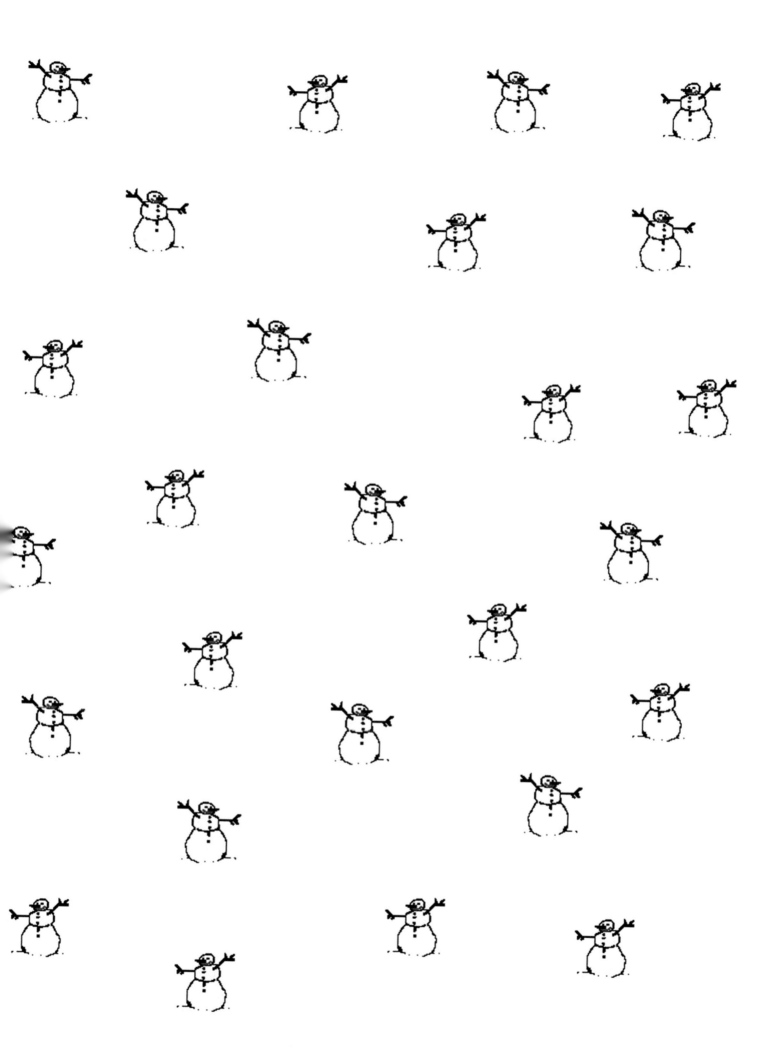

Printed in the United States
by Baker & Taylor Publisher Services